T0196005

# INTRODUCTION TO
# ORACLE
# DATABASE
## ADMINISTRATION

## YING WANG

**author**HOUSE®

*AuthorHouse™*
*1663 Liberty Drive*
*Bloomington, IN 47403*
*www.authorhouse.com*
*Phone: 1 (800) 839-8640*

*Published by AuthorHouse  01/15/2020*

*ISBN: 978-1-7283-4326-6 (sc)*
*ISBN: 978-1-7283-4357-0 (e)*

# ACKNOWLEDGEMENTS

I would like to thank my co-workers Masud Salahuddin, Shannon Tulk and Carrie Vifansi etc. who helped me and supported me in my works. Without them I cannot finish this book. I also want to thank my family to support my jobs.

# CONTENTS

# CHAPTER 1

# INTRODUCTION TO DATABASE MANAGEMENT SYSTEM

## 1.1 What Is Database Management System

A database management system (DBMS) is system software for creating and managing databases. The DBMS provides users and programmers with a systematic way to create, retrieve, update and manage data.

The DBMS manages three important things: the data, the database engine that allows data to be accessed, locked and modified -- and the database schema, which defines the database's logical structure. These three foundational elements help provide concurrency, security, data integrity and uniform administration procedures. Typical database administration tasks supported by the DBMS include change management, performance monitoring/tuning and backup and recovery. Many database management systems are also responsible for automated rollbacks, restarts and recovery as well as the logging and auditing of activity.

## 1.2 Popular RDBMS in the World

Most popular RDBMS in the world is Oracle, MS Sql Server and IBM DB2. Others include My Sql, Access, Sybase etc.

## Oracle

Oracle database is the most widely used object-relational database management software. Developed in 1977. The latest version of this tool is 12c where c means cloud computing. It supports multiple platforms like Windows, UNIX, and Linux versions.

## IBM DB2

Latest release 11.1. Developed in the year 1983. The language used is Assembly Language, C, C++ for writing it. It supports multiple Windows, UNIX, and Linux versions.

## Microsoft Sql Server

Developed in the year 1989. Latest updated version came in 2016. The language used is Assembly C, Linux, C++ for writing it.
Works on Linux and windows operating system.

# 1.3   Database and Application

A DBMS makes it possible for end users to create, read, update and delete data in a database. The DBMS essentially serves as an interface between the database and end users or application programs, ensuring that data is consistently organized and remains easily accessible.

Database usually is on the database server (backend) and application is on the frontend. An application can be on either a user's desktop or on an application server which depends on the application system architecture design. Usually for a web based application (multitier), application is on application server or web server and non-web based application, application is installed on desktop.(client-server architecture).

## Clients

A client initiates a request for an operation to be performed on the database server. The client can be a Web browser or other end-user process. In a multitier architecture, the client connects to the database server through one or more application servers.

## Application Servers

An application server provides access to the data for the client. It serves as an interface between the client and one or more database servers, which provides an additional level of security. It can also perform some of the query processing for the client, thus removing some of the load from the database server.

The application server assumes the identity of the client when it is performing operations on the database server for that client. The application server's privileges are restricted to prevent it from performing unneeded and unwanted operations during a client operation.

## Database Servers

A database server provides the data requested by an application server on behalf of a client. The database server does all of the remaining query processing.

The Oracle database server can audit operations performed by the application server on behalf of individual clients as well as operations performed by the application server on its own behalf. For example, a client operation can be a request for information to be displayed on the client, whereas an application server operation can be a request for a connection to the database server

# CHAPTER 2

# ORACLE DATABASE MANAGEMENT SYSTEM

## 2.1    Oracle Database System Architecture

Oracle database system architecture include physical storage structure and logical storage structure. Physical storage structure are files on server including data files, control files, redo logfiles. Logical storage structure includes schema objects which are tables, views, indexes, database triggers, stored procedures, tablespaces etc. logical objects in Oracle database.

## 2.2    Database Administrators vs Database Developers

A database Administrator's major jobs are creating and setting up and maintaining physical storage structures. It includes installing Oracle software, setting up Oracle instance, performance monitoring/ tuning, backup/recovery database etc. A database developer's jobs are creating and setting up and maintaining logical storage structures. It includes designing and creating and maintaining tables, indexes, triggers and stored procedures, views etc. and data maintaining like data loading, inserting, deleting and updating etc. In this book, the major contents are Oracle database administration not database development. One exception is that tablespace is logical object but tablespace management is DBA job.

## 2.3   Oracle Database Server Structure

An Oracle database server consists of an Oracle database and an Oracle instance. Every time a database is started, a system global area (SGA) is allocated and Oracle background processes are started. The combination of the background processes and memory buffers is called an Oracle instance.

# CHAPTER 3

# ORACLE DATABASE CREATION AND UPGRADE

---

## 3.1  Oracle Database Creation Method

### 3.1.1  Install Oracle software

Download Oracle software first from Oracle website and install it. Oracle has different version and edition like 12c,11G,10g. Enterprise edition and standard edition etc.

### 3.1.2  Create System Database

After creating Oracle database, you have system tablespace, data dictionary, sys and system user, temporary tablespace undo tablespace etc. physical and logical structures.

Create Oracle database using DBCA(GUI)

The Database Configuration Assistant (DBCA) Creation Mode window enables you to create a database with default configuration or to use Advanced Mode to create a database.

If you choose **Advanced Mode**, you can customize storage

locations, initialization parameters, management options, database options, and different passwords for Administrator user accounts.

If you choose **Create a database with default configuration**, you make fewer choices in the options for your database, which allows you to create your database sooner.

When you select **Create a database with default configuration**, you can select the following options:

**Global Database Name**: Enter the database name in the form *database_name.domain_name.*

**Storage Type**: Choose either **File System** or **Automatic Storage Management**.

When you choose **File System**, your database files are managed by the file system of your operating system.

When you choose **Automatic Storage Management**, you place your data files in Oracle Automatic Storage Management (Oracle ASM) disk groups.

**Database Files Location**: The choice you make for the **Storage Type** option determines what you specify for the **Database Files Location** option.

When you choose **File System** in the **Storage Type** field, you specify the directory path where the database files are to be stored in the **Database Files Location** field. Oracle Database can create and manage the actual files.

When you choose **Automatic Storage Management** in the **Storage Type** field, you specify the disk group to use in the **Database Files Location** field (the disk group must already exist). With Oracle ASM, Oracle Database automatically manages database file placement and naming.

**Fast Recovery Area**: Specify a backup and recovery area.

**Database Character Set**: Choose the character set to use for the database.

### 3.1.3   Create listener and net service name

After creating Oracle database instance, you need to create listener. On the database host, the Oracle Net listener (the listener), is a process that listens for client connection requests. It receives incoming client connection requests and manages the traffic of these requests to the database server.

The default listener configuration file is called listener.ora, and it is located in the network/admin subdirectory of the Oracle home directory.

Configuring Listening Protocol Addresses Using Oracle Net Manager
The following procedure describes how to configure protocol addresses for the listener using Oracle Net Manager:

1.   Start Oracle Net Manager.
2.   In the navigator pane, expand **Local**, and then select **Listeners**.
3.   Select the listener.
4.   From the list in the right pane, select **Listener Locations**.
5.   Select the protocol from the Protocol list.
6.   Enter the host name for the listener in the Host field.
7.   Enter the port number in the Port field.
8.   If you want to set send and receive buffer sizes, then click **Show Advanced**, and then enter the sizes in the appropriate fields.
9.   Select **Save Network Configuration** from the File menu to save the changes.

### 3.1.4   Start Up and Stop listener

Starting or Stopping a Listener Using the Listener Control Utility

To start the listener from the command line, enter:

```
lsnrctl START [listener_name]
```

In the preceding command, *listener_name* is the name of the listener defined in the listener.ora file. It is not necessary to identify the listener if you are using the default listener name LISTENER. In addition to starting the listener, the Listener Control utility verifies connectivity to the listener.

To stop a listener from the command line, enter:

```
lsnrctl STOP [listener_name]
```

In the preceding command, *listener_name* is the name of the listener defined in the listener.ora file. It is not necessary to identify the listener if you are using the default listener name LISTENER.

### 3.1.5   Create application database

An application database usually is a data repository for a specific application like property tax assessment application, document management application etc. usually DBA create an application owner user first, the application admin uses this user to connect to Oracle database to create application logical structures like tables, indexes, views, triggers, stored procedures etc. One application can have one or more schemas. One application or more applications can share one Oracle instance. It depends on application size and management method.

## 3.2  Oracle Database Upgrade Method

### 3.2.1  DBUA upgrade

This is the most often use method. It is a GUI method so it is easy. The limit is this method is only fit only same OS platform upgrade.

1.  Read readme before upgrade
2.  Install high version Oracle software
3.  Bring up DBUA, step by step upgrade Oracle DB

### 3.2.2  EXPDP/IMPDP upgrade

This method can be used for different OS platform. For example from Windows to Unix or vice versa.
ExpDP/IMPDP can also use for logical backup/recover for Oracle database.

For example:
set oracle_home=c:\oracle\DbSrv12cR2\FLX51\OraSoft
expdp system/Pwd@ORCL schemas=TAXDBA exclude=table:\"in (\'GM_DOCUMENTS\',       \'TX_ACCTS_JN\',\'TX_ERRORS\',\'TX_ADDRS_JN\',\'GM_ASSET_DETAILS\')\" DIRECTORY =data_pump dumpfile=expdp_taxdba_nofive_documents.dmp logfile=expdp_taxdba_nofive_tables.log
Above expdp script export all tables and data and other logical objects in ORCL instance for taxdba user but not including some big tables.

set oracle_home=c:\oracle\DbSrv12cR2\FLX51\OraSoft
impdp taxdba/pwd@ORCL tables=tx_rep_transactions_2012 table_exists_action=truncate dumpfile= data_pump:expdp_flextest_table.dmp logfile=data_pump:impdp_flexprod_table.log

Above impdp script import table tx_rep_transactions_2012 data in ORCL taxdba user. The dump file is expdp_flextest_table.dmp.

# CHAPTER 4

# ORACLE DATABASE DESIGN AND DATA MANAGEMENT

## 4.1 Table and Column and Table Relationship

Tables are the basic unit of data storage in an Oracle Database. Data is stored in rows and columns. You define a table with a table name, such as employees, and a set of columns. You give each column a column name, such as employee_id, last_name, and job_id; a datatype, such as VARCHAR2, DATE, or NUMBER; and a width. The width can be predetermined by the datatype, as in DATE. If columns are of the NUMBER datatype, define precision and scale instead of width. A row is a collection of column information corresponding to a single record.

You can specify rules for each column of a table. These rules are called integrity constraints. One example is a NOT NULL integrity constraint. This constraint forces the column to contain a value in every row.

After you create a table, insert rows of data using SQL statements. Table data can then be queried, deleted, or updated using SQL.

For example, in Employee table, you have five employees. Susan, Joe, John, April and Shannon. There are five columns in this table. Emp_No, Name, Brith Date, Sex, Department. This table stores basic employee information. The first row is column, and other rows are data.

| Emp_no | Name | Birth Date | Sex | Department |
|--------|------|------------|-----|------------|
| 1 | Susan | Dec 5 1970 | F | Finance |
| 2 | Joe | Jan 20 1965 | M | Finance |
| 3 | John | Mar 7 1982 | M | HR |
| 4 | April | May 2 1972 | F | IT |
| 5 | Shannon | Aug 9 1975 | M | IT |

Two tables may have relationship. For example, one department can have one or many employees but one employee can only belongs to one department, so department table and employee table is one to many relationship.

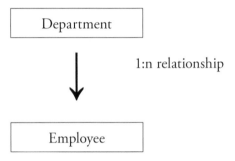

So in Employee table, you can have a foreign key column called dept_no, which data must be in Department table.

| Dept_no | Dept_name |
|---------|-----------|
| 1 | IT |
| 2 | Finance |
| 3 | Engineering |
| 4 | HR |

In Employee table

| Emp_No | Name | Birth Date | Sex | Dept_no |
|--------|------|------------|-----|---------|
| 1 | Susan | Dec 5 1970 | F | 2 |
| 2 | Joe | Jan 20 1965 | M | 2 |

| 3 | John | Mar 7 1982 | M | 4 |
| 4 | April | May 2 1972 | F | 1 |
| 5 | Shannon | Aug 9 1975 | M | 1 |

Table Department is master table, table employee is details table.

Each table can have a primary key which is one or many columns which determined one row in the table like dept_no can be primary key in department table while emp_no can be primary key in employee table.

## 4.2 Data and Data type

Each column has a data type like integer, number, varchar2,Date, Blob etc. Once data type is defined only this data type data can be inserted, others are invalid. Also you can have constraints to define data range. For example, you can define each column can only have certain values or Null or not Null data.

## 4.3 SQL language

SQL language is Query Structure Language which is a basic language for database. You use this language as an interface to operate data like insert data, delete or update data. Also you can use it to select data(query) or create/drop tables, users etc. Both developers and DBAs use SQL to access database.

Select Statement like:
Select Emp_no, Name from emp where emp_no < 3;
Insert statement like:
Insert into emp values(6,'Richard','Dec 7 1977','M',1);
Update statement like:
Update EMP set Brith_date='Nov 7 1977' where emp_no=6;
Delete statement like:
Delete Emp where emp_no=6;
Create table statement like:

Create table EMP (emp_no integer primary key, name varchar2(20), Brith_date Date, Sex char(1),dept_no integer);

## 4.4 PL/SQL language

Oracle PL/SQL is an extension of SQL language, designed for seamless processing of SQL statements enhancing the security, portability, and robustness of the database.

Similar to other database languages, it gives more control to the programmers by the use of loops, conditions and object-oriented concepts.

## 4.5 Tablespace and Data Dictionary

### 4.5.1 What is Tablespace

Tablespace is a logical concept which is a group of same type of database objects like tables, indexes etc. storage space. One tablespace can contain one or many data files on different drives. Once an Oracle database is created, there are several default tablespaces. They are:

SYSTEM Tablespace----Super user SYS's objects, user SYSTEM's objects

SYSAUX Tablespace-----Other system default users objects like

UNDO Tablespace-----Undo segments

Temp Tablespace-----temporary tables, group by etc aggregated statement in select tables, insert/delete operation needs creating temporary tables

User Tablespace-----any other user's objects

Tools Tablespace----any tools user's objects

### 4.5.2 What is Data Dictionary

Data dictionary is Oracle system tables and views which belongs super user SYS. With these views, DBA or users can get application objects information in database like table name, view name, column name etc. meta data information. There are 3000 DBA_

data dictionary views in Oracle 12c. User's data dictionary is user_
xxxx. The major data dictionary for DBA include:

dba_users---- all user's name and password etc. info

dba_roles---- all roles name and other information

dba_tables----all tables in Oracle database.

Dba_indexes---all indexes data

Dba_views-----all views information

Dba_objects---all objects data including table, index, stored procedures, stored functions, synonyms, views etc

dba_tab_columns---tables and columns and data type information

dba_tablespaces---tablespace name, block size, extent information

dba_tab_privs—table name, owner, grantee, privileges

dba_data_files---data file name, file id, tablespace name, bytes etc

except DBA_ view, there are also some dynamic data dictionary view like

v$instance display instance information

v$logfile identify redo log group, log members and status

When you type desc data dictionary name like desc dba_tables, it shows dba_tables structures like column name, size etc.

For example: desc dba_users

VIEW dba_users

| Name | Null? | Type |
|---|---|---|
| USERNAME | NOT | NULL VARCHAR2(128) |
| USER_ID | NOT | NULL NUMBER |
| PASSWORD | | VARCHAR2(4000) |
| ACCOUNT_STATUS | NOT | NULL VARCHAR2(32) |
| LOCK_DATE | | DATE |
| EXPIRY_DATE | | DATE |
| DEFAULT_TABLESPACE | NOT | NULL VARCHAR2(30) |

| Name | Null? | Type |
|---|---|---|
| TEMPORARY_TABLESPACE | NOT | NULL VARCHAR2(30) |
| LOCAL_TEMP_TABLESPACE | | VARCHAR2(30) |
| CREATED | NOT | NULL DATE |
| PROFILE | NOT | NULL VARCHAR2(128) |
| INITIAL_RSRC_ CONSUMER_GROUP | | VARCHAR2(128) |
| EXTERNAL_NAME | | VARCHAR2(4000) |
| PASSWORD_VERSIONS | | VARCHAR2(17) |
| EDITIONS_ENABLED | | VARCHAR2(1) |
| AUTHENTICATION_TYPE | | VARCHAR2(8) |
| PROXY_ONLY_CONNECT | | VARCHAR2(1) |
| COMMON | | VARCHAR2(3) |
| LAST_LOGIN TIMESTAMP(9) | | WITH TIME ZONE |
| ORACLE_MAINTAINED | | VARCHAR2(1) |
| INHERITED | | VARCHAR2(3) |
| DEFAULT_COLLATION | | VARCHAR2(100) |
| IMPLICIT | | VARCHAR2(3) |
| ALL_SHARD | | VARCHAR2(3) |

## 4.6 Oracle Database Initialization Parameters

All database initialization parameters are contained in either an initialization parameter file (PFILE) or a server parameter file (SPFILE). As an alternative to specifying parameters in an initialization parameter file or server parameter file, you can modify dynamic parameters at runtime using the ALTER SYSTEM SET or ALTER SESSION SET statements.

There are default initialization parameters and you can change them. When starting up an Oracle instance, Oracle read initialization file.

Location of the Initialization Parameter File

If you do not specify a different initialization file with option PFILE at database startup, then by default Oracle Database uses initialization parameter files located in

*ORACLE_HOME*\Database\init.ora

For Example:

audit_file_dest= 'C:\Oracle\DbSrv12cR2\FLX81\admin\flextest\ adump'

audit_trail='db'
compatible='12.2.0'
control_files='D:\Oracle\DbSrv12cR2\FLX81\Oradata\flextest\ control01.ctl'
db_block_size=8192
db_name='flextest'
db_recovery_file_dest='G:\Oracle\DbSrv12cR2\FLX81\FRA\ flextest'
db_recovery_file_dest_size=161061273600
diagnostic_dest='C:\Oracle\DbSrv12cR2\FLX81'
dispatchers='(PROTOCOL=TCP) (SERVICE=flextestXDB)'

nls_language='AMERICAN'
nls_territory='AMERICA'
open_cursors=300
pga_aggregate_target=4096m
processes=320
remote_login_passwordfile='EXCLUSIVE'
SGA_MAX_SIZE=16384M
sga_target=16384m

undo_tablespace='UNDOTBS2'

with Pfile, you can create SPFILE. For example use the following sql create spfle from pfile='c:\oracle_home\database\initflextest.ora'; you create a spfile called spfileflextest.ora in c:\oracle_home\database. Spfile is binary and cannot be edited from file level, you can alter system to set parameter in spfile. Pfile can be edited.

E.G alter system set undo_tablespace='UNDOTBS1' scope=spfile;

Also database parameters can be selected using v$parameter dynamic data dictionary.

desc v$parameter

VIEW v$parameter

| Name | Null? | Type |
|------|-------|------|
| NUM | | NUMBER |
| NAME | | VARCHAR2(80) |
| TYPE | | NUMBER |
| VALUE | | VARCHAR2(4000) |
| DISPLAY_VALUE | | VARCHAR2(4000) |
| DEFAULT_VALUE | | VARCHAR2(255) |
| ISDEFAULT | | VARCHAR2(9) |
| ISSES_MODIFIABLE | | VARCHAR2(5) |
| ISSYS_MODIFIABLE | | VARCHAR2(9) |
| ISPDB_MODIFIABLE | | VARCHAR2(5) |
| ISINSTANCE_MODIFIABLE | | VARCHAR2(5) |
| ISMODIFIED | | VARCHAR2(10) |
| ISADJUSTED | | VARCHAR2(5) |
| ISDEPRECATED | | VARCHAR2(5) |
| ISBASIC | | VARCHAR2(5) |
| DESCRIPTION | | VARCHAR2(255) |
| UPDATE_COMMENT | | VARCHAR2(255) |
| HASH | | NUMBER |
| CON_ID | | NUMBER |

# CHAPTER 5

# ORACLE DATABASE BACKUP AND RECOVER

## 5.1 What is Database Backup and Recover

Database backup is a method to backup database files or data to another device either tape or backup servers/disks in case a recover during disaster.

## 5.2 Oracle Database Backup and Recover Methods

Oracle provide two type of backup/recover methods. They are physical backup/recover and logical backup/recover. Logical backup is online hot backup. Physical backup has cold and hot backup two types. Hot backup means database does not need to shut down, application is online when backup is going. Cold backup means a database shutdown is needed before doing a backup.

## 5.3 Physical Backup and Recover

Physical backup/recover is backup database physical files like data files, control files, log files etc. and recover them.
In Physical backup/recover, there are two methods. One is RMAN backup/recover and another is user management backup recover. RMAN is an Oracle tools which provide a RMAN language to backup/recover database files. This method is automatic backup

method. RMAN is Recover Manager. User Management backup/ recover is using OS command to copy database files.

Logical backup is using EXPDP tool to backup database logical structures like tablespace, tables, data, stored procedures, indexes etc.

Backup strategy is depended on user requirement of application and database type like Production, Test or Development database. If an application is 24 by 7 online critical application, you can only choose online hot backup method. If your application requires data loss is 2 hours, you need to backup archive log files every 2 hours. For Test or Dev database, you can choose cold backup weekly or daily and choose put database in nonarchivelog mood.

## 5.4 User Management Backup and Recover

### 5.4.1 User Management Backup

User Management backup method is to use OS command to do a hot or cold database backup. For cold backup, shutdown instance first, then copy all database files to backup folder. You can also copy pfile and spfiles, control file text format, password files to backup folder too. Then bring up the database instance.

For example, a script for cold backup database test

```
SET ECHO OFF
SET HEADING OFF
SET VERIFY OFF
SET FEEDBACK OFF
SET LINESIZE 200
SET DEFINE ON
DEFINE dbName = 'test'
DEFINE bkpDir = 'G:\Oracle\DbSrv12cR2\FLX51\Backups\
Physical\test'

alter system checkpoint;
host del /q &bkpDir\*.*
create pfile = '&bkpDir\pfile_&dbName..txt' from spfile;
```

alter database backup controlfile to trace as '&bkpDir\ctlfile_
&dbName..txt';
spool &bkpDir\bkpDbFiles.bat
SELECT 'xcopy '||value||' &bkpDir\ /V /Y' FROM v$parameter
WHERE name='spfile';
SELECT 'xcopy '||name||' &bkpDir\ /V /Y' FROM v$controlfile;
SELECT 'xcopy '||name||' &bkpDir\ /V /Y' FROM v$datafile;
SELECT 'xcopy '||member||' &bkpDir\ /V /Y' FROM v$logfile;

spool off

shutdown immediate;

host call &bkpDir\bkpDbFiles.bat;
host del &bkpDir\bkpDbFiles.bat;

startup

exit

For example, a script for hot backup database test:
SET ECHO OFF
SET HEADING OFF
SET VERIFY OFF
SET FEEDBACK OFF
SET LINESIZE 200

SET DEFINE ON

DEFINE dbName = 'test'
DEFINE bkpDir = 'G:\Oracle\DbSrv12cR2\FLX51\Backups\
Physical\test'

alter system checkpoint;

host del /q &bkpDir\*.*

```
create pfile = '&bkpDir\pfile_&dbName..txt' from spfile;
alter database backup controlfile to trace as '&bkpDir\ctlfile_
&dbName..txt';

spool &bkpDir\bkpDbFiles.bat
SELECT 'xcopy '||value||' &bkpDir\ /V /Y' FROM v$parameter
WHERE name='spfile';
SELECT 'xcopy '||name||' &bkpDir\ /V /Y' FROM v$controlfile;
SELECT 'xcopy '||name||' &bkpDir\ /V /Y' FROM v$datafile;
SELECT 'xcopy '||member||' &bkpDir\ /V /Y' FROM v$logfile;

spool off

alter database begin backup;

host call &bkpDir\bkpDbFiles.bat;
host del &bkpDir\bkpDbFiles.bat;

alter database end backup;
alter system switch logfile;
alter system switch logfile;
alter system switch logfile;

exit
```

In hot backup, you do not need to shutdown database, just need to put database in backup mode. The database files are not writable during the backup mode and the changes are stored in the SGA, redo logs and Rollback segments. And these changes will be the written into the data files when the database is taken out of begin backup mode.

### 5.4.2   User Management Database Recover

Database recover method is depended on backup method. If it is cold backup, recover method is simple, just copy data files backup to original locations and startup database. If it is hot backup, recover steps are as following:

a.  Copy back all the online datafile from backup location to the actual datafile location.

b.  Copy back control file to all the controlfile locations, refer controlfile locations from parameter file, i.e. initRTS.ora file.

c.  Copy back pfile or spfile file to its location.

d.  Startup database in mount mode: startup mount

recover database with the help of following command and specify log: AUTO. SQL> recover database until cancel using backup controlfile;

ORA-00279: change 1117103 generated at 07/12/2017 04:39:47 needed for thread 1

ORA-00289: suggestion : /home/oracle/archdir/1_90_910140016. dbf

ORA-00280: change 1117103 for thread 1 is in sequence #90

Specify log: {<RET>=suggested | filename | AUTO | CANCEL}

AUTO

e.  Open database with resetlogs: SQL> alter database open resetlogs;

## 5.5  RMAN Backup and Recover

RMAN is an oracle auto backup/recover tool. It provides a RMAN command language to auto backup/recover database.

For example, a full online backup script is as following:

set oracle_sid=test
rman target / catalog rman/rman@oemrep CMDFILE rman_wholebk_out.txt LOG rman_wholebk.log
rman_wholebk_out.txt is:

```
run
{
backup incremental level=0 database ;

}
```

The following is RMAN script for cold incremental backup.

```
run {
shutdown immediate;
startup mount;
backup incremental level=1 cumulative database;
sql 'alter database open';}
```

## 5.6   EXPDP/IMPDP Backup and Recover

EXPDP is a logical backup tool which backup database logical structures like tables, data, indexes, stored procedures etc. It is an online backup method but for IMPDP recover, it is an offline recover.

For example, the following Windows script is a full backup script using expdp for a test database.

```
SET ORACLE_HOME=C:\Oracle\DbSrv12cR2\FLX51\OraSoft
SET ORACLE_SID=TEST
SET sstPwd=Orcl2018%
SET dpDir=data_pump
SET      dmpSfx=%date:~2,2%%date:~5,2%%date:~8,2%_
%time:~0,2%%time:~3,2%

del/Q   G:\Oracle\DbSrv12cR2\FLX51\Backups\DataPump\
TEST\*.*

EXPDP system/%sstPwd%@%ORACLE_SID% ^
DIRECTORY=%dpDir% ^
FULL=y ^
```

DUMPFILE=%ORACLE_SID%_full_%dmpSfx%.dmp ^

LOGFILE=%ORACLE_SID%_full_%dmpSfx%.log

With EXPDP, you can back up the whole database, one or more schemas, one or more tables in one schema etc. It is a very flexible Oracle logical backup tool.

# CHAPTER 6

# ORACLE DATABASE REFRESH

## 6.1   What is Oracle Database Refresh

Oracle database refresh is also called Oracle database clone. It usually means refresh development or test database from production database. So that Test or DEV database has same data with production database. It is a regular job for DBA. Database refresh is based on backup/recover theory and methods.

## 6.2   User Management Physical Backup and Refresh Method

Physical backup/refresh method is using user management physical backup/recover method to do a database refresh.

The step is:

1.   do 'alter database backup controlfile to trace' on production DB. Find control file creation script in udump, rename it to sid_control.sql
2.   cold backup production DB
3.   create directories on test box for test DB(oradata\new_ sid, admin\new_sid\udump, pfile, scripts, bdump, cdump, archive, exp, oracle\backup\new_sid)
4.   copy DB files to new location on test box(oracle\oradata\ NEW_SID\)

5. copy and rename initSID.ora PWDSID.ora, sid_control.sql to new location on test box(oracle\ora92\database\pwdnew_sid.ora)

6. modify initNEW_SID.ora, keep db_name and instance_name as the old one and only modify location.

7. create a new db service by doing

   oradim –new –sid new_sid –startmode auto

8. set oracle_sid=new_sid

9. sqlplus /nolog

10. connect / as sysdba

11. startup mount pfile=$ORACLE_BASE\admin\new_sid\pfile\initnew_sid.ora

12. run renamedbfiles.sql script to rename the location of the DB files, keep the DB name as production one.

13. shutdown immediate

14. modify initNEW_SID.ora and NEW_SID_control.sql, replace SID to NEW_SID and modify location(remove startup nomount, remove recover database, resetlog if it is a new database, use reuse set database to rename DB names, change DB name to a new one)

15. startup nomount pfile=new_sid pfile

16. recreate controlfile by doing @$ORACLE_BASE\admin\new_sid\scripts\new_sid_control.sql create spfile(create spfile='c:\oracle\ora92\database\spfileNEW_SID.ora' from pfile='c:\oracle\admin\NEW_SID\pfile\initNEW_SID.ora')

17. shutdown immediate

18. startup

19. backup the new DB

## 6.3  RMAN Backup and Refresh Method

Refresh test database FLEXTEST from production database FLEXPROD script example is as following:

connect target sys/pwd@flexprod

```
connect catalog rman/pwd1@rmanprod
run

{sql 'alter system switch logfile';}

connect auxiliary sys/pwd2@flextest

run
{
allocate auxiliary channel a1 device type disk;

set newname for datafile
'I:\oracle\DB11gR2_FLX_P1\oradata\flexprod\system01.dbf' to
'I:\oracle\DB11gR2_FLX_T1\oradata\flextest\system01.dbf';

set newname for datafile
'F:\oracle\DB11gR2_FLX_P1\oradata\flexprod\undotbs02.dbf' to
'F:\oracle\DB11gR2_FLX_T1\oradata\flextest\undotbs02.dbf';

set newname for datafile
'd:\oracle\DB11gR2_FLX_P1\oradata\flexprod\tools01.dbf' to
'd:\oracle\DB11gR2_FLX_T1\oradata\flextest\tools01.dbf';

set newname for datafile
'd:\oracle\DB11gR2_FLX_P1\oradata\flexprod\users01.dbf' to
'd:\oracle\DB11gR2_FLX_T1\oradata\flextest\users01.dbf';

set newname for datafile
'd:\oracle\DB11gR2_FLX_P1\oradata\flexprod\gamma_data01.
dbf' to
'd:\oracle\DB11gR2_FLX_T1\oradata\flextest\gamma_data01.dbf';

set newname for datafile
'd:\oracle\DB11gR2_FLX_P1\oradata\flexprod\tax_data.dbf' to
'd:\oracle\DB11gR2_FLX_T1\oradata\flextest\tax_data.dbf';
```

```
set newname for datafile
'd:\oracle\DB11gR2_FLX_P1\oradata\flexprod\tax_data02.dbf' to
'd:\oracle\DB11gR2_FLX_T1\oradata\flextest\tax_data02.dbf';

set newname for datafile
'e:\oracle\DB11gR2_FLX_P1\oradata\flexprod\tax_index_02.dbf' to
'E:\oracle\DB11gR2_FLX_T1\oradata\flextest\tax_index_02.dbf';

set newname for datafile
'e:\oracle\DB11gR2_FLX_P1\oradata\flexprod\gamma_index01.
dbf' to
'E:\oracle\DB11gR2_FLX_T1\oradata\flextest\gamma_index01.
dbf';

set newname for datafile
'I:\oracle\DB11gR2_FLX_P1\oradata\flexprod\sysaux01.dbf' to
'I:\oracle\DB11gR2_FLX_T1\oradata\flextest\sysaux01.dbf';

set newname for tempfile
'I:\oracle\DB11gR2_FLX_P1\oradata\flexprod\temp01.dbf' to
'I:\oracle\DB11gR2_FLX_T1\oradata\flextest\temp01.dbf';

duplicate target database to flextest until time 'sysdate - 0.005'
logfile
group 1
('H:\oracle\DB11gR2_FLX_T1\oradata\flextest\redo01.log')
size 100m,
group 2
('H:\oracle\DB11gR2_FLX_T1\oradata\flextest\redo02.log')
size 100m,
group 3
('H:\oracle\DB11gR2_FLX_T1\oradata\flextest\redo03.log')
size 100m;
}
```

## 6.4   EXPDP backup and Refresh Method

1. Use expdp to backup database
2. Create a new database instance
3. Use impdp to import all data and structure. Application user and tablespace will be created in impdp procedures.

# CHAPTER 7

# ORACLE DATABASE SECURITY

## 7.1    What is Oracle Database Security

Database security entails allowing or disallowing user actions on the database and the objects within it. Oracle uses schemas and security domains to control access to data and to restrict the use of various database resources.

Oracle provides comprehensive discretionary access control. **Discretionary access control** regulates all user access to named objects through privileges. A privilege is permission to access a named object in a prescribed manner; for example, permission to query a table. Privileges are granted to users at the discretion of other users.

## 7.2    Oracle Database Users and Schemas

In Oracle database, users can be created by SYSTEM and SYS users which are Oracle default system users with DBA privileges. Usually use SYSTEM user to create an application DBA for one application. Use this application DBA to create other users in the application like in Flexsuite application we create a application DBA called TAXDBA which has DBA role. SYS user is the owner of data dictionary with sysdba role. All system data dictionary belongs to user SYS. So usually we only use SYS to do startup/shutdown, backup etc server side DBA jobs. Other work we use user SYSTEM or application DBA user TAXDBA to do them to avoid creating any application objects in SYS schema or make mistakes in data dictionary.

Each user has a same name schema. Schema is a set of tables, indexes, views, stored procedures etc. database objects. One application can have only one or many schemas which depends on application database design method. One application one schema method is simpler to maintain. One user can only have one schema.

## 7.3   Oracle Database Roles

Oracle database roles is a set of privileges. Each role has a role name and a set of privileges. One user can have one or many roles. One role can be granted to one or many users. Of cause one user can be granted privileges directly too but usually we use roles to grant privileges to users to limit users access to tables in database and ensure database security.

The following script can get all users and their roles in a specific user profile:

select grantee, granted_role from dba_role_privs where grantee not in (select role from dba_roles) and grantee in
(select username from dba_users where profile='FLEXSUITE_ USERS') order by grantee;

## 7.4   Oracle Database Privileges

Oracle database privileges is operations user or role can have. These privileges include system level privileges such as select all dictionary, select any tables, create any tables. The privileges also include application level privileges which means user or role can only have access to application's schema not the whole system level. Such as select emp, update emp, delete emp or insert emp. Emp is a table name etc. DBA of application creates roles and users and also can grants privileges and roles to roles and users.

The following script can get all roles and privileges they have in a specific schema TAXDBA which is application Flexsuite schema and owner user.

select grantee,owner,table_name,privilege,grantor from dba_tab_ privs where owner='TAXDBA' and grantee not in

(select username from dba_users) order by grantee;

## 7.5    Oracle Database Profiles

An Oracle **profile** is a set of limits on database resources. If you assign the profile to a user, then that user cannot exceed these limits.

Oracle Database enforces resource limits in the following ways:

- If a user exceeds the CONNECT_TIME or IDLE_TIME session resource limit, then the database rolls back the current transaction and ends the session. When the user process next issues a call, the database returns an error.
- If a user attempts to perform an operation that exceeds the limit for other session resources, then the database aborts the operation, rolls back the current statement, and immediately returns an error. The user can then commit or roll back the current transaction, and must then end the session.
- If a user attempts to perform an operation that exceeds the limit for a single call, then the database aborts the operation, rolls back the current statement, and returns an error, leaving the current transaction intact.

Usually we have DBA profile, application profile, default profile which is Oracle provided profile. All DBA users are assigned to DBA_PROFILE. Different users can be assigned to different application user profiles like FLEXSUITE_USERS profile, DEV_ USERS_PROFILE, TRANSFER_USER_PROFILE etc. Use create profile statement to create a profile and use create or alter user statement to assign a user to a profile.

For Example:

```
CREATE PROFILE FLEXSUITE_USERS LIMIT
SESSIONS_PER_USER UNLIMITED
CPU_PER_SESSION UNLIMITED
CPU_PER_CALL UNLIMITED
CONNECT_TIME UNLIMITED
IDLE_TIME UNLIMITED
LOGICAL_READS_PER_SESSION UNLIMITED
LOGICAL_READS_PER_CALL UNLIMITED
COMPOSITE_LIMIT UNLIMITED
PRIVATE_SGA UNLIMITED
FAILED_LOGIN_ATTEMPTS 10
PASSWORD_LIFE_TIME 45
PASSWORD_REUSE_TIME 365
PASSWORD_REUSE_MAX 24
PASSWORD_LOCK_TIME 1
PASSWORD_GRACE_TIME 30
PASSWORD_VERIFY_FUNCTION    ORA12C_VERIFY_
FUNCTION;
```

ORA12_Verify_Function is defined password complexity policy for Flexsuite user password. Oracle has a default password policy but you can modify this script to set up your password complexity policy. This password complexity function belongs to SYS.

Password complexity rule in our application Flexsuite is:

1. At least 8 characters
2. Must contain one Capital letter
3. Must contain one number

4.  Must contain one special
5.  Password should differ 3 characters than old password

The script for ORA12_verify_function is:

```
CREATE OR REPLACE FUNCTION SYS.ora12c_verify_
function
(username varchar2,
password varchar2,
old_password varchar2)
RETURN boolean IS
differ integer;
db_name varchar2(40);
i integer;
reverse_user dbms_id;
canon_username dbms_id := username;
BEGIN
-- Bug 22369990: Dbms_Utility may not be available at this point,
so switch
-- to dynamic SQL to execute canonicalize procedure.
IF (substr(username,1,1) = '"") THEN
execute immediate 'begin dbms_utility.canonicalize(:p1, :p2, 128);
end;'
using IN username, OUT canon_username;
END IF;

IF NOT ora_complexity_check(password, chars => 8, UPPER =>
1, digit => 1,
special => 1) THEN
RETURN(FALSE);
END IF;

-- Check if the password contains the username
IF regexp_instr(password, canon_username, 1, 1, 0, 'i') > 0 THEN
raise_application_error(-20002, 'Password contains the username');
END IF;
```

```
-- Check if the password contains the username reversed
FOR i in REVERSE 1..length(canon_username) LOOP
reverse_user := reverse_user || substr(canon_username, i, 1);
END LOOP;
IF regexp_instr(password, reverse_user, 1, 1, 0, 'i') > 0 THEN
raise_application_error(-20003, 'Password contains the username' ||
'reversed');
END IF;

-- Check if the password contains the server name
select name into db_name from sys.v$database;
IF regexp_instr(password, db_name, 1, 1, 0, 'i') > 0 THEN
raise_application_error(-20004, 'Password contains the server
name');
END IF;

-- Check if the password contains 'oracle'
IF regexp_instr(password, 'oracle', 1, 1, 0, 'i') > 0 THEN
raise_application_error(-20006, 'Password too simple');
END IF;

-- Check if the password differs from the previous password by at
least
-- 3 characters
IF old_password IS NOT NULL THEN
differ := ora_string_distance(old_password, password);
IF differ < 3 THEN
raise_application_error(-20010, 'Password should differ from the'
|| 'old password by at least 3 characters');
END IF;
END IF ;

RETURN(TRUE);
END;
```

Above script is an update of Oracle default ORA12_Verify_function.

# CHAPTER 8

# ORACLE DATABASE TROUBLE SHOOTING

## 8.1 Oracle Error and Log Files

Oracle has an error number ORA-xxxxxx to show Oracle errors. Also Oracle provides an alert log files, listener log file, tracing files etc. to track database activities and errors. Alert log file name is ORA_SID.ora.

- Alert log
  Need to check regularly to see if any errors in DB, find ORA- errors
  Need to rename online manually if it is too big.
  Location is $Oracle_BASE\diag\rdbms\SID\SID\trace\alert_SID.log

- Listener log
  Need to check for trouble shooting
  Need to rename manually offline if it is too big (shutdown listener first)
  Location is
  $ORACLE_BASE\diag\tnslsnr\$host_name\$listener_name\trace\$listener_name.log

- Trace files
  Need to remove manually every year
  Location is $Oracle_BASE\diag\rdbms\sid\sid\trace\*.trc

## 8.2   How to Handle Oracle Errors

The following method can be used to fix ORA- errors.

- Google ORA-error messages, find solution there which is simplest method.
- Find Ora-error and solution from Oracle Error reference book online documentation.
- Put questions on Oracle technique network(www.oracle.com)
- Open a service request in Oracle support website to get help from Oracle support(metalink.oracle.com)

# CHAPTER 9

# ORACLE DATABASE REGULAR MAINTENANCE

## 9.1 Regular Health Check and Maintenance Jobs

As a DBA, you need to do a regular database health check to keep database healthy including

### 9.1.1 Check index fragmentation and defrag if needed

Script to check index fragmentation and defrag it is as following:

```
set serveroutput on
declare
v_count number;

Begin
FOR INDEx_RECORD IN (select index_name as obj
from dba_indexes
where index_type ='NORMAL' and
owner ='TAXDBA'
) LOOP
execute immediate 'analyze index '|| INDEx_RECORD.obj ||'
compute statistics';
```

execute immediate 'analyze index '|| INDEx_RECORD.obj ||'
validate structure';
select count(name) into v_count from index_stats where (lf_rows
> 100 and del_lf_rows
> 0)
and (height > 3 or ((del_lf_rows/lf_rows)*100) > 20);
if v_count > 0
then
begin
dbms_output.put_line('ALTER INDEX '||INDEx_RECORD.
obj||' REBUILD;');

execute immediate 'ALTER INDEX '||INDEx_RECORD.obj||'
REBUILD';
end;
end if;
END LOOP;
END;-- implicit CLOSE occurs

### 9.1.2    Check **TEMP, UNOD** tablespace size, if too big resize them

Check UNDO tablespace size, if over 1G shrink it to 100M. script
is as following:

CREATE SMALLFILE UNDO
TABLESPACE "UNDOTBS1"
DATAFILE

'D:\ORACLE\DbSrv12cR2\FLX51\ORADATA\FLEXPROD\
UNDOTBS01.DBF' SIZE
100M AUTOEXTEND
ON NEXT 1M MAXSIZE 32767M;
alter system set undo_tablespace = undotbs1;
drop tablespace undotbs2 including contents and datafiles;
alter tablespace undotbs1 rename to undotbs2;
shutdown immediate

startup mount

rename filename on drive D—OS lever

alter database rename file 'D:\ORACLE\DbSrv12cR2\FLX51\ ORADATA\FLEXPROD\UNDOTBS01.DBF' to 'D:\ORACLE\ DbSrv12cR2\FLX51\ORADATA\FLEXPROD\UNDOTBS02. DBF';

alter database open;

Check temp tablespace size, if over 1G shrink it to 500M

- Create temporary tablespace TEMP1
- Set TEMP1 default temporary tablespace
- Drop TEMP
- Create TEMP
- Set TEMP default temporary tablespace
- Drop TEMP1

If drop temp tablespace is hang, issue select username,session_ num,session_addr from v$sort_usage where tablespace='TEMP; Select sid,serial#,status from v$session where serial#=session_num; Alter system kill session 'sid,serial#' immediate;

For Example:

CREATE TEMPORARY TABLESPACE TEMP2 TEMPFILE 'D:\Oracle\DbSrv12cR2\FLX51\Oradata\Flexprod\TEMP02. DBF'

SIZE 500M REUSE AUTOEXTEND ON NEXT 1M MAXSIZE 32767M;

ALTER DATABASE DEFAULT TEMPORARY TABLESPACE TEMP2;

SELECT b.tablespace,b.segfile#,b.segblk#,b.blocks,a.sid,a.serial#, a.username,a.osuser, a.status

FROM v$session a,v$sort_usage b

WHERE a.saddr = b.session_addr;

If sessiom 133,63386 is result of above select statement, then issue: alter system kill session '133,63386';

DROP TABLESPACE TEMP including contents and datafiles;
CREATE TEMPORARY TABLESPACE TEMP TEMPFILE 'D:\Oracle\DbSrv12cR2\FLX51\Oradata\Flexprod\TEMP01. DBF'
SIZE 500M REUSE AUTOEXTEND ON NEXT 1M MAXSIZE 32767M;
ALTER DATABASE DEFAULT TEMPORARY TABLESPACE TEMP;
DROP TABLESPACE TEMP2 including contents and datafiles;

**9.1.3** Check alert log regular to see if there are ora-errors need to be fixed.

**9.1.4** Use other DBA tools like **TOAD DB** health check function to see if there are other database design issues.

## 9.2 Database Management System Monitoring

There are some tools to do database monitoring works like Solarwinds DPA, Oracle Enterprise manager 12c. It can monitor instance up/down, performance issues, CPU, DISK Network, memory etc. resource usage, index fragmentation, tablespace full, alert log error etc. Also it can give advice like index advice and SQL analysis report.

# CHAPTER 10

# DATABASE ADMINISTRATION STANDARD

## 10.1  Naming Convention

One kind of database design and management standard is naming convention including database server name, Oracle home name, table name, tablespace name, index name, stored procedure name, username, role name etc. To define a naming convention is very good for managing a database which makes everything clear and easy to manage.

For example:

Server name ORC5v01, ORC5v02, ORC8v01, ORC8v02

ORC-----Oracle DB

5---production DB, 8---test DB,7 –dev DB,6—training DB 4---sandbox DB etc.

01,02 is sequence number.

Instance name: FLEXPROD,FLEXTEST,FLEXDEV means FLEX*SUITE application Prod, test and dev instance.

Table Name: TX_ACCTS, TX_LINCS means tax table, FS_

View Name:TX_V_FILING,TX_V_LAND_USE_MILL,GM_ V_BUILDING

Oracle Home Name: ORACLE_HOME=C:\Oracle\ DbSrv12cR2\FLX81\OraSoft

Oracle_HOME=C:\Oracle\DbSrv12cR2\FLX51\OraSoft

FLX51 means Flexsuite app production database, FLX81 means

Flexsuite app Test database. DbSrv12CR2 means Oracle database server 12c R2.

## 10.2   Request For Change Management (RFC)

RFC is another database management standard regarding changes. Usually errors come from changes, so change control is very important in practice. RFC process includes:

- Change request and reason for change(new patches, new functions, database upgrade, application upgrade, system integrations etc.)
- Record change in ticketing system like KACE or others
- Business tests changes in test environment and write test plan and result
- Change implementation plan
- RFC approve by supervisor or an RFC committee

With RFC change management process, change errors in production system can be reduced to minimum.

# REFERENCES

Oracle Database Online Documentation 11*g* Release 2 (11.2)
Database Administration

Printed in the United States
By Bookmasters